Tokenizing Sports

The Rise of Crypto-Centric Teams, Leagues, and Platforms

Table of Contents

Chapter 1. Introduction

In the thrilling intersection of sports and technology, an extraordinary innovation is taking the field - the world of sports is taking a transformative leap through the inception of crypto-centric teams, leagues, and platforms. This Special Report "Tokenizing Sports: The Rise of Crypto-Centric Teams, Leagues, and Platforms" delves deep into this groundbreaking juncture. It uncovers how traditional sports is undergoing a vibrant metamorphosis, subtly integrating cutting-edge cryptology. It doesn't matter if you're a techno savvy sports enthusiast or just a casual spectator, this comprehensive report will captivate your interest, revealing how avid fans now have the opportunity to own a piece of their favorite teams via crypto tokens and how sporting leagues are reshaping their financial landscape. You'll be instilled with a fresh understanding and possibly, a burning curiosity to become a part of this pioneering venture. Purchase this special report to venture into this exhilarating playing field where technology and sports converge in unprecedented ways.

Chapter 2. The Junction of Sports and Cryptocurrency

The new millennium has transformed the world of technology in ways previously unimagined, but it has also fervently stirred the sports echelon, directing it towards uncharted territories. This transformation began subtly but has quickly become a full-fledged revolution with the advent of cryptocurrencies.

2.1. Understanding Cryptocurrencies

Originally, cryptocurrency burst onto the scene as a financial tool away from governmental regulation. With the invention of Bitcoin, the world forayed into a new era of digital finance. Cryptocurrencies work using technology called blockchain, a decentralized system spread across many computers that manages and records transactions.

Though born within the financial realm, the applications of blockchain and cryptocurrency are numerous, breaching various sectors, including sports. The decentralized and transparent nature of the technology offers solutions to some of the sports industry's most chronic issues while also creating new opportunities for growth and development.

2.2. Sports Say Hello to Crypto

The adoption of crypto technologies in the world of sports has been gradual but consistent. Several clubs across different sports initiated this integration on trial bases, slowly witnessing incremental benefits. Case in point, teams such as the Sacramento Kings of the

NBA began accepting Bitcoin for ticket and merchandise purchases as far back as 2014. This progressive move turned heads, inspiring many more to follow suit.

Over the last few years, there's been an explosive burst of activity in the area of sports and crypto, with a focus on tokenization. By offering fungible digital tokens, teams can now monetize their brand and engage with their fans worldwide. These tokens give fans a degree of ownership and numerous other benefits, leading to an increased sense of affinity and loyalty towards the team.

2.3. Fan Tokens Take the Field

Fan tokens have been a breakout phenomenon in the football world. Socios.com, fronted by blockchain firm Chiliz, has taken the lead in this space. The platform allows fans to acquire fan tokens of some of the most prominent football clubs globally like Juventus, Paris Saint-Germain, and FC Barcelona.

These crypto tokens serve multiple purposes. They give fans voting rights on certain club decisions: which message the captain wears on the armband, music the stadium plays when the team scores a goal, and other club-related trivial matters. Token holders also access exclusive merchandise, unique experiences, and other perks. Essentially, these tokens bring fans closer, nurturing a never-before experience of involvement and participation.

2.4. Blockchain Management of Merchandising

Merchandising is a significant revenue stream for sports clubs, but counterfeiting is a critical issue. Here, blockchain serves as the perfect solution due to its digital ledger system.

Several sports outfits are turning towards blockchain to solve this.

NBA, for instance, has launched a digital platform for fan engagement where they can exchange official digital goods, creating a marketplace for unique items. Such platforms ensure the merchandise's authenticity and provide an extra layer of trust and confidence for the consumer.

2.5. Smart Contracts and Player Transfers

Beyond merchandising and engagement, blockchain's applications extend to contract management, especially in player transfers in sports like football. Traditional paper contracts are susceptible to forgery, disputes, and misinterpretation. But blockchain-based smart contracts ensure better transparency, reducing disputes.

Blockchain brings fairness, transparency, and efficiency to the complex transfer process by embedding terms of agreement within the system, executing them automatically when the conditions are met. Clubs, players, and agents can view the terms accurately, eliminating potential misunderstandings or disputes.

2.6. Crypto Sponsorships

Engaging with cryptocurrency has also redefined sports sponsorships. As cryptocurrencies gain mainstream acceptance, sports outfits are partnering with crypto firms for sponsorships. Premier partners, kit sponsors, or name rights sponsors - cryptocurrency companies are making a mark everywhere.

2.7. The Road Ahead

No one can definitively predict what the future holds for the intersection of sports and cryptocurrency. Challenges abound - regulation, market volatility, and public understanding. However, the potential benefits are too promising to dismiss.

The advent of crypto and sports convergence is a thrilling prospect, fueling fan passion while making sports more interactive and enjoyable. This intersection has unlocked a new frontier, and it might be just the beginning of an unprecedented journey. Technology has been a game-changer for sports for centuries, and crypto seems set to be the next chapter in this ongoing saga.

Chapter 3. The Emergence of Crypto-Centric Teams

In recent years, the sports industry has become increasingly engrossed with an unlikely collaborator - cryptocurrencies. Just like any other industry that has embraced digital innovation, the sports industry is experiencing a significant transformation with the inception of crypto-centric teams.

3.1. The Dawn of Crypto Sponsorships

The first signs of crypto's integration in sports could be traced back to when crypto exchanges and companies began sponsoring teams in various sports leagues globally. Crypto companies like eToro and StormGain made significant partnerships in the football industry, notably with teams such as Tottenham Hotspur, Leicester City, and Newcastle United, among others. These sponsorships entail inscriptions of the exchange logos on the playing kits and offering exclusive online promotions. The strategic angle to this was simple: as millions of fans across the globe watch these teams play, the brands of these crypto companies become subtlety embedded in their consciousness. With time, these sponsorships grew more elaborate, graduating into full-fledged partnerships where the crypto platforms offered services directly related to the sporting activities.

3.2. Rise of Fan Tokens

One of the major breakthroughs that have marked the emergence of crypto-centric teams is the innovative idea of Fan Tokens. These are specific types of cryptocurrency tokens linked to a particular team or club. Created on blockchains, they provide an avenue for interaction between fans and their favorite teams beyond mere support. Owning a fan token gives a fan voting rights on some club decisions, VIP experiences, exclusivity to merchandise, and more. Socios.com, a blockchain-based app that facilitates fan engagement, has been instrumental in the creation and management of such fan tokens for teams like FC Barcelona, Paris Saint-Germain, Juventus, among others.

3.3. Blockchain Alliance

The potential of blockchain in the sports industry is enormous. Recognizing this, some sports franchises have formed direct alliances with blockchain platforms to explore possibilities beyond fan tokens. For instance, the Sacramento Kings, a franchise in the National Basketball Association (NBA), allied with ConsenSys, a blockchain software technology company, to launch a new auction platform that fans can use to bid on authentic memorabilia and unique game-worn gear. All the auctions will be implemented using Treum, an Ethereum-based platform.

3.4. Cryptocurrency Payments

Another significant development in the establishment of crypto-centric teams is the acceptance of cryptocurrencies as a means of payment. NFL player Russell Okung made headlines when he announced that he would receive half of his $13 million salary in bitcoin, making him one of the first significant athletes to adopt cryptocurrency. Furthermore, the Dallas Mavericks became the first NBA team to accept Bitcoin as a method of payment for match tickets and merchandise.

3.5. Player Tokenization

The integration of cryptology in sports has also spawned an entirely new concept of player tokenization. Using this innovative model, athletes can issue their tokens to their fans, providing them the opportunity to buy stakes in their future income, including signing bonuses, salaries, sponsorship deals, and more. This novel idea blurs the line between traditional sports fandom and financial speculation and has generated heated debates within the sports and crypto community. Spencer Dinwiddie, an NBA player, was among the first to lead this initiative.

3.6. The Future of Crypto-Centric Teams

As blockchain continues to infiltrate the sports industry, the emergence of crypto-centric teams indicates a new era of fan engagement, fundraising, and player contracts. But just as vital is the profound change it will bring to the financial architecture. It can also take player autonomy to a new level where they can have financial control and authority that has been far-fetched.

It's clear that this is just the beginning - we are yet to see the culmination of this transformative fusion. As more teams fall into the crypto bandwagon and more fans get awakened to the reality of being a part of their beloved teams, there's neither doubt that crypto-centric teams will continue to rise, nor that their impact will be multidimensional. At the same time, it's assuring that the dynamism of technology will not leave sports behind. This synergy between sports and technology is surely an intriguing aspect to watch as we move forward into the future of sports.

Chapter 4. Revamping Sports Leagues through Cryptocurrency

The sports industry, in its ceaseless quest for innovation and improvement, has always been a frontrunner in integrating popular trends and technologies, and cryptocurrency, in recent years, has emerged as a game-changer in this domain. The remarkable fusion of sports and cryptocurrency is dramatically redefining the industry, with sports leagues across the globe undergoing a radical transformation, shifting traditional business models towards a more dynamic and inclusive future.

4.1. Introducing Cryptocurrencies and Blockchain in Sports

Cryptocurrencies, digital or virtual currencies that operate on the principles of cryptography, along with related technologies like blockchain, have stormed the global finance sector, setting off ripples across various industries. They've successfully penetrated the sports arena too, becoming an unprecedented force of change.

Sports leagues have started to appreciate the resilience, flexibility, and inclusivity embedded within cryptocurrencies and blockchain technology. This shift isn't merely limited to implementing tech-savvy payment methods but extends to redefining how a team interacts with its fan-base, manages its finances, and even inducts new players.

4.2. Decentralization as a Game Changer

A critical facet of cryptocurrencies that makes them attractive for sports leagues is the idea of decentralization. Unlike traditional currencies where financial institutions regulate the dynamics of transactions, cryptocurrencies operate on a decentralized network. This structure introduces a wellspring of advantages like transparency and direct peer-to-peer interactions, which are transforming the world of sports by democratizing various processes.

For sports leagues, decentralization means that fans are no longer bystanders; they can take an active part in their favorite team's affairs via FTOs (Fan Token Offerings). These tokens provide fans unprecedented access, allowing them to participate in decisions like jersey designs, team logos, and even pre-season schedules. This novel convergence of sports and blockchain technology evolves the fan-club relationship into a more egalitarian, interactive, and exciting dynamic.

4.3. Tokenization of Athletes and Teams

While fan engagement is one facet of this astonishing amalgamation, the notion of tokenizing athletes and teams marks another groundbreaking trend. Teams are now issuing crypto tokens representing fractional ownership of a player's potential earnings or a portion of a team. It's equivalent to a virtual stock market, where fans and investors can trade tokens representing their favorite players or teams, providing a novel route of revenue for athletes and sports organizations.

Besides adding a financial dimension to fandom, this model allows underprivileged athletes to raise funds directly from their admirers and investors, overriding the traditional, and often daunting, funding routes. Athletes can tokenize their contracts, pledges, or performance bonuses, selling a portion to the highest bidders and raising essential funds for their professional growth.

4.4. The Road to Financial Diversity

For sports leagues, integrating with cryptocurrency opens up a plethora of financial opportunities. Staging matches, player contracts, maintenance of stadiums, and managing staff require a colossal amount of funding - and cryptocurrency provides a new avenue to meet these financial expectations. League administrations aren't confined to traditional methods of revenue generation (like ticket sales, merchandise, and broadcasting rights); they can experiment with NFTs, tokens, and various blockchain-based opportunities to add new revenue streams.

Additionally, introducing cryptocurrencies into the mix enables sports leagues to reach global audiences beyond geographical constraints. It also standardizes processes by having a common, universally accepted mode of transaction, removing the friction of currency conversion and international transfers involved in traditional monetary systems.

4.5. Conclusion

The amalgamation of sports leagues and cryptocurrency, although still nascent, is promising a radical and vibrant transformation. The opportunities stemming from this convergence are multifold, from altering the dynamics of fan interactions, providing funding routes for athletes, to adding new revenue streams for leagues and organizations. Despite the regulatory and implementation challenges, this avant-garde blend of sports and technology is steadily moving towards becoming an integral part of the global sports paradigm.

As more people dive into this dynamic mix of sports and cryptocurrencies, the boundaries of what is possible in the realm of sports are likely to be challenged and redefined. And with it, the vibrant and fervent world of sports enthusiasts, athletes, and leagues will be served a thrilling spectacle that goes beyond the pitch, court, or stadium, into the exciting digital world of blockchain and cryptocurrencies.

Unquestionably, in this brave new world of sports, whoever embraces these cutting-edge technologies stand to redefine the game - not just play it.

Chapter 5. Platform Revolution: Blockchain at Play

There's hardly a field remaining untouched by blockchain, and sports is no exception. This digital, distributed, immutable ledger is playing a pivotal role in shifting paradigms across the sports industry, proving its abilities far beyond its original financial application.

5.1. Blockchain Basics

The concept of blockchain, as part of Distributed Ledger Technology (DLT), sprouted from the implementation of digital cryptocurrency, Bitcoin. As the underlying technology, blockchain provided a tamper-proof and transparent way to record transactions. But its utility extends well beyond cryptocurrencies.

Comprising blocks of data linked via cryptographic principles, the blockchain is an open, verifiable system. Once the data is recorded, it becomes nearly impossible to change, fostering transparency. The decentralized nature distributes power and function across the network instead of centralizing it, fostering a system of trust and security.

5.2. Blockchain in the Sports Industry

What does this high-powered technology mean for the world of sports? Quite a lot. Blockchain is disrupting the traditional conduits of sporting organizations, athletes, fans, commercial partners, and more. It heralds a new era of unprecedented fan engagement, fairer remuneration models, and unexploited potent commercial opportunities.

Among the notable shifts blockchain technology nurtures in the sports industry, the role of fans is experiencing a paradigmatic change. The power dynamic has long been unidirectional, with teams and clubs controlling every aspect of the game. Blockchain, however, offers a chance to redistribute this power and create a circular ecosystem where fans, too, can partake in decision-making processes or benefit financially.

5.3. Tokenizing Sports Assets

Moreover, with the help of blockchain, sports-related assets can be tokenized, and these tokens can democratize the ownership of sports entities. The token economy offers fans a completely new way to engage with their favorite clubs - they can acquire voting rights on certain issues, or even own a small percentage of an organization.

The French football club, Paris Saint-Germain (PSG), for instance, leveraged the flexibility of tokenization to launch its Fan Token Offering (FTO). These tokens give holders the right to vote on various club-specific matters and a sense of ownership. Implementation of this model by the Juventus club follows similar lines. These examples illustrate how blockchain technology is enabling clubs to innovate their relationship with fans while infusing additional funds into the ecosystem.

5.4. Counterfeit Merchandise

Blockchain also promises to curtail a long-standing plague in the sports industry - counterfeit merchandise. By assigning each piece of merchandise a unique blockchain-based identity, it becomes impossible to replicate, allowing brands to guarantee authenticity.

VeChain's ToolChain is an excellent example of this system in action, making it easier and more cost-effective for businesses and teams to verify and track batches of products across supply chains.

5.5. Revolutionizing Sports Betting

For bookmakers and bettors, blockchain provides a transformative influence. Smart contracts - self-executing contracts with the terms directly written into the code - can ensure fairness, transparency, and immediacy. Thus, bets can automatically pay out based on real-world data inputs without requiring intermediaries to verify the results.

5.6. Ensuring Athlete Compensation

In various sports, unfair compensation has been a pressing issue. Blockchain technology could edge away such disparities, ensuring fair compensation for athletes. Tokenization of contracts and performances, combined with blockchain's transparency, means deals can be scrutinized publicly. This would ensure fair pay and may even lead to bonuses for performance-based milestones.

5.7. Final Thoughts

Blockchain is clearly not just a speculative phenomenon in the world of finance. Its integration in the sports sector is a testament to its diverse potential applications. Whether it's democratization and fan engagement, combating counterfeit merchandise, transforming betting, or assuring fair pay to athletes, blockchain ticks all the boxes for a technological revolution in the sports industry. Its implementation unleashes the potential to reshape the entire sporting eco-system, forging a new model of trust, transparency, and engagement. Thus, we are truly witnessing a "Platform Revolution," with blockchain taking the lead in the game.

Chapter 6. Spearheading Crypto Engagement: Fan Tokens

In the picturesque panorama of sporting action, the rambunctious cheers of enthusiastic fans form the throbbing heartbeat. In recent years, the advent of blockchain technology and cryptocurrencies has opened newer avenues for clubs and franchises to engage their supporters more actively, transforming a mere spectator sport into an immersive and interactive engagement. Central to this dynamic paradigm shift are fan tokens, which are swiftly becoming an integral part of sports' captivating orchestra.

6.1. Creating a Bond: What are Fan Tokens?

Fan tokens are digital assets made using blockchain technology that provides fans with a real, tangible way to influence their favourite clubs or teams. These crypto-based tokens are generally minted on platforms like Chiliz, Socios, and others, depending on partnerships with sports teams, leagues or clubs.

The value proposition these tokens provides is multifold. Not only do they serve as a ticket to augmented fan experiences, but they also double as potential investment tools. When a fan purchases these tokens, they earn the power to vote in polls about the club's affairs and access exclusive merchandise, content, VIP experiences, games, and much more.

Another captivating factor about fan tokens is their tradability on crypto exchanges, hence showing potential for appreciation in value. Applauding goals on the pitch may fetch symbolic joy, but witnessing a tangible asset tied to your favorite team rise in value delivers an exhilarating experience.

6.2. Empowering Fans: How Fan Tokens Transform Engagement?

Taking a closer look at how fan tokens have been redefining sports and the fan experience, one can rightly validate the adage 'Money can't buy happiness, but it can buy fan tokens.'

The line between fans and clubs has been blurring with the evolution of an all-new fan engagement model that puts fans at the helm of matters. Fan tokens are becoming a gateway to exclusive club decisions, ranging from choosing the club's jersey, crest redesign, charity initiatives, to even deciding friendly match opponents.

Teams, clubs, and franchises, in their turn, benefit immensely from their augmented engagement, fostering a tighter bond with their existing supporters, and attracting a newer, tech-savvy, audience.

6.3. The Financial Ramifications: Fan Tokens and Revenue Generation

On the financial front, fan tokens have proven to be a lucrative venture for clubs and franchises alike. Parma Calcio 1913, an Italian Serie C football team, reportedly generated revenues of €250,000 in just 24 hours after launching their fan tokens. The potential revenue from fan tokens for clubs is effectively limitless, as they create new and diverse revenue streams that were previously untapped.

Another crucial facet is the stability offered by the shift towards fan token, especially for clubs seeking financial sustainability in the face of dwindling ticket sales and reduced physical attendances due to COVID-19 restrictions. In such circumstances, fan tokens provide an alternative revenue channel, independent of the thrills and spills on the pitch.

Moreover, the substantial revenue generated from these fan tokens go a long way in keeping the clubs financially robust, allowing them to invest in infrastructure, players, and backroom staff to remain competitive.

6.4. The Risks and Challenges

However, as with any disruptive technology or concept, the incorporation of fan tokens is not devoid of hurdles. Skepticism about the volatility of the token value and their dependence on market fluctuations is a dominant concern. Besides, the novel concept demands intensive educational campaigns to help sports fans understand the perks and pitfalls of fan tokens.

Lack of robust regulation is another concern that feeds uncertainty. Although self-regulating bodies exist within the crypto market, governments, and international organizations are yet to establish comprehensive guidelines to safeguard investors.

6.5. Cases in Point: Successful Adoption of Fan Tokens

An insight into successful adoptions of fan tokens can effectively underline their potential to rearchitect sports engagement. Examples from European Football giants like FC Barcelona, Paris Saint-Germain, and Juventus indicate the successful execution of fan tokens.

FC Barcelona's fan token ($BAR) sale raised $1.3million in just two hours, while Paris Saint-Germain saw $PSG prices soaring by 80%

following Messi's transfer announcement.

It's worth noting that not only football clubs are partaking in this trend but also sports like MMA and eSports, drawing in a fresh wave of fan engagement and participation.

It's clear – fan tokens are a sea change for sports fans, clubs, and the wider sporting ecosystem. However, it is essential to trim the edges of associated risks and provide clear regulatory frameworks to build trust amongst fans and investors. Successful adoption will require an amalgamation of efforts from sports institutions, regulatory bodies, and supporters alike. These three actors of the dramatic play of sports, when come together, can effectively write a new saga of fan engagement and rejuvenate the thrill of sports.

Chapter 7. Financial Rewiring: From Traditional Investment to Tokenization

History seems to teeter on the brink of vibrant transition with the introduction of financial technologies. The sports industry, though traditionally resilient to rapid change, finds itself at the heart of this technological revolution. Privatization and traditional investment models have long dominated the sports finance landscape. However, with the growing adaptation of blockchain technology, tokenization promises to carve a fresh path for the industry, gradually dissolving the boundaries of the existing financial backdrop.

7.1. The Dawn of Privatization

Sports teams have, traditionally, relied on wealthy individuals or corporations to finance their operations and ride the turbulent waves of the market. No instance underlines this better than the championships-driven spending by sports tycoons. Sports privatization traced back to the late 19th century, as local business magnates began to see the financial viability in supporting hometown sports teams.

In the modern era, we see even more quantum leaps. Take, for instance, the National Football League (NFL) in the United States. In 1994, the average NFL team was just worth $175 million. Fast forward to 2019, and the average valuation of NFL teams soared to $2.86 billion, marking an unprecedented compound annual growth rate of 11.6%. A similar trend is observed across major global sports leagues, signifying the harness of privatization.

7.2. Changing Notions of Investment

And yet, the traditional model of owning sports teams, with its allure, is often out of reach for the vast majority. For those who lack the financial robustness, participating in the sporting economy constitutes buying merchandise or tickets. However, fans have often wondered: wouldn't it be captivating to actually own a part of their favorite team?

A solution first came into sight with fan-owned teams such as F.C Barcelona and Green Bay Packers. Then entered an innovative form of crowd-funding: tokenization, built on the bedrock of blockchain technology.

7.3. A Primer to Blockchain and Crypto Tokens

Blockchain technology, in simple terms, is a type of database storage system. It stores information in blocks that are then chained together. As new data comes in, it is entered into a new block that gets chained to the previous block.

Crypto tokens represent a particular fungible and tradable asset or a utility created over a blockchain. These token models have the potential to induce dramatic changes in the traditional sports financing system by introducing a democratised form of trading and investment.

7.4. Moneyball: Tokenization Style

Tokenization leverages the security of blockchain technology and has the potential to completely revolutionize sports financing, bringing about greater financial inclusivity and fan engagement.

Creating a digitized economy around league and team tokens will allow fans to participate in micro-investments. Through tokenization, fans can buy a piece of their sports team or players they believe in, rallying behind them not just emotionally, but financially too.

Furthermore, these tokens may well hold real-world utilities, such as voting rights on team decisions or discounts on merchandise and ticket purchases, nudging the boundaries of fan engagement even further.

7.5. Tokens and Leagues: A Reimagined Financial Landscape

Beyond the view of transforming sports team ownership and fan engagement, tokenization can be a fundamental tool for sports leagues across the world for raising investment and managing finances. Sports leagues could generate tokens which can then be sold to investors on a blockchain platform. The resulting ecosystem would yield increased transparency and reduced instances of fraud, thanks to the decentralized, immutable nature of blockchain.

The capital raised through tokenization could help leagues fund talent development, capitalize on digital platforms, and finance infrastructural enhancements. This will potentially lead to a more vibrant, competitive, and global sports landscape.

7.6. The Future Looks 'Tokenized'

While we are still early in the journey of sport tokenization, and hurdles around regulation, adoption and trust remain to be crossed, it's clear that blockchain has opened up a brand new playing field. The financial structures surrounding sports that have long felt immovable are now fluid. Blockchain has the potential to rewire sports finance from the ground up, shaping a more inclusive and engaging future for one of the world's most beloved pastimes.

Chapter 8. Legal Implications and Regulatory Challenges

Enlightening themselves on the potential legal implications and regulatory challenges is essential for stakeholders interested in crypto-centric sports platforms. Although tokenizing sports brings about a sea change in engagement and financial structures, overcoming legal and regulatory hurdles is a prerequisite for long-term success.

8.1. Understanding Regulatory Frameworks

Implementing cryptocurrency into the sporting landscape requires understanding existing regulatory frameworks. Each country has its unique laws surrounding cryptocurrencies. As such, teams, leagues, and platforms must familiarize themselves with specific regulations in their operational jurisdictions.

In the U.S, for instance, the Securities and Exchange Commission (SEC) oversees most instances of token issuance, closely scrutinizing whether they qualify as securities. The 1946 Supreme Court ruling in the SEC v. Howey case forms the basis of what constitutes a 'security'. As per this ruling, investments of money in a venture with an expectation of profits predominantly from the efforts of others were recognized as securities. Tokens that meet this 'Howey Test' would fall under the regulatory oversight of the SEC.

Large sporting leagues have a global presence, with fans located across multiple jurisdictions. Therefore, the regulatory framework becomes a complex tapestry of laws, rules, and regulations. Compliance is absolutely crucial and can impact an entity's growth strategy.

8.2. Tokenizing Assets and Securities Law

With fans becoming investors through the purchase of tokens, teams have to ensure they aren't unknowingly issuing securities. Understanding how property rights translate onto a blockchain could vary between jurisdictions. For instance, owning a 'share' of a team might imply different legal responsibilities depending on the country.

Apart from the legal implications of managing property rights, there are potential tax implications too for fans who purchase tokens. For instance, capital gains tax could apply depending on the change in value of tokens held. Several jurisdictions might classify tokens as assets, while some might consider them as intangible property. It becomes critical for the stakeholders to comprehend the legal nuances.

8.3. Money Laundering and Terrorism Financing

Cryptocurrencies' potential misuse for money laundering or terrorism financing is also a significant issue that regulators worry about. Due to the inherent anonymity possibility, cryptocurrencies can be exploited by malicious agents. Hence, organizations that tokenize their assets might need to incorporate preventative measures such as Know Your Customer (KYC) and Anti-Money Laundering (AML) procedures to mitigate such risks.

8.4. Smart Contracts and Dispute Resolution

Smart contracts form the backbone of tokenized systems. As automated self-executing contracts with the terms of the agreement directly written into code, they provide the mechanism for token transactions. However, the nascent nature of this technology brings with it several legal implications.

For instance, in the case of disputes arising from the smart contract execution, it could be challenging to establish jurisdictions in a blockchain's decentralized setup. Furthermore, the liability questions in case of a smart contract failure could arise. Legislations to control, supervise and guide the usage of smart contracts may be potentially enacted to address this 'legal limbo'.

8.5. Overcoming The Hurdles

Legal and regulatory challenges, although seem daunting, as illustrated above, are not insurmountable. Proactive engagement with legal experts and regulatory authorities to understand the changing legal landscape can provide clarity. Despite its potential problems, tokenizing sports has transformative potential, and hence it is worth overcoming the challenges it brings along.

This wave of tokenization is driving the sports industry to unchartered territories, requiring a delicate balance between leveraging opportunities and managing potential risks. With adequate due diligence and legal planning, the sports world can indeed embrace this shift toward the exciting world of cryptocurrencies. The key lies in understanding the divide between the physical and digital arenas, knowing how to bridge the gap sustainably and legally.

Chapter 9. Pushing Boundaries: Case Studies of Crypto in Sports

As the intersection of sports and technology becomes increasingly intertwined, the emergence of cryptocurrency turns the traditional business model of sports on its head. Driven by the promise of decentralization, enhanced transactional speed, increased security, and broadened accessibility, cryptocurrencies are gradually gaining adoption in the sports industry, unlocking new opportunities for athletes, fans, clubs, and sponsors alike.

9.1. Entering the pitch: Clubs and Digital Currencies

Sporting teams and leagues worldwide have begun to experiment with cryptocurrencies and blockchain technology to innovative ends. One notable adopter is the famed Italian football club, Juventus. In 2019, they launched their fan token ($JUV), hoping to foster a more interactive relationship with their global fan base. The token allows holders to vote on certain club matters, like theme songs and kit designs, thereby creating a more immersive fan experience.

Now extending beyond mere fan engagement, these digital tokens are also gradually reshaping club finances. Recently, Paris Saint-Germain (PSG) struck a unique deal with cryptocurrency exchange platform Crypto.com. In exchange for a significant sponsorship sum, PSG received payment partially in cryptocurrency. Deals like these signify new ways crypto is changing traditional sports sponsorship and payment mechanisms.

9.2. A New Era of Fan Engagement

Across multiple sports, clubs and leagues are leveraging the democratizing and interactive capabilities of crypto tokens to provide unprecedented fan engagement opportunities. Spain's leading football club, FC Barcelona, launched its fan token ($BAR), facilitating innovative digital interactions. Token holders can participate in diverse decision-making processes, from choosing inspirational locker room quotes to the walkout anthem played at home games, offering fans a more intimate connection with the club than ever before.

In the NBA, the landmark collaboration between Dapper Labs and the league gave birth to NBA Top Shot, a platform where fans can buy, sell, and trade officially licensed NBA collectible highlights, referred to as 'Moments.' These Moments, stored as Non-Fungible Tokens (NFTs), provide fans with digital ownership of iconic game instances, capturing and capitalizing on the passion and nostalgia inherent in sports fandom. The NBA Top Shot marketplace has seen over $700 million in sales since its launch in 2020, proving the powerful allure of blockchain-meets-sports.

9.3. Contractual Innovation and Player Empowerment

Cryptocurrency is also offering an avenue for players to broaden their income streams and retain greater control over their image rights. NFL player Russell Okung became one of the first professional athletes to be paid in Bitcoin, sparking significant attention in traditional and social media.

Likewise, NBA player Spencer Dinwiddie took the lead in space innovation, tokenizing his contract to offer accredited investors a share in his future earnings, thereby creating a bond-like mechanism to leverage his future success. These novel applications of cryptocurrency within sports contracts illustrate its potential to revolutionize traditional player financing models.

9.4. The Rise of Crypto-Centric Leagues

The growing wave of crypto integration into sport has also led to the creation of entirely new, crypto-centric leagues and teams. The new blockchain-based sport, Socios United Leagues (SUL), is funded by fan token purchases. It is a global, de-centralized league where fans, depending upon their token investments, have decision-making powers that once lay solely in the hands of team owners and managers. In this bold transformation, fans become integral participants in the sport, their decisions shaping the future of the teams and the games themselves.

Likewise, in the world of e-sports, the convergence of blockchain and gaming has given rise to crypto-centric teams. Teams such as Team Heretics in Spain have released their crypto Tokens, allowing global supporters to participate and vote in key decisions, thereby shaping their favorite teams' destiny.

9.5. Investment and Sponsorship Opportunities

In addition to enabling new forms of fan engagement and innovative business models, cryptocurrency also opens up fresh investment opportunities. Crypto companies are increasingly targeting sports for advertising and sponsorship, viewing it as an excellent platform to reach a wider audience.

Against this backdrop, the influx of major sponsors from the crypto world is elevating the financial potential of sports considerably.

Crypto.com, for example, recently signed a historic deal worth $100 million to sponsor the prestigious Formula 1 races. Such partnerships undoubtedly amplify the crypto brands' visibility while simultaneously injecting considerable resources into the sporting leagues.

9.6. Future Perspectives

As the boundaries of what's possible in sport continue to be rewritten, the integration of cryptology in sports clubs, leagues, and platforms signals an exciting sea change. The pioneering examples of Juventus, FC Barcelona, and NBA Top Shot, among others, illuminate the path for future innovation.

Yet, for all the promising strides, it is essential to remember that the adoption of cryptocurrency in sports is still in its relatively early stages. Future growth will likely depend on evolving regulatory environments, technology advancements, and broadened public acceptance of cryptocurrencies. Nevertheless, the pace of change is without a contemporary correlate, promising a future of endless possibilities in the world of sport.

Chapter 10. Future Projections: Tokenizing Sports in the Coming Years

The strategic blend of blockchain technology and sports is revolutionizing the industry, providing a myriad of possibilities and pushing the boundaries of fan engagement, team ownership, and revenue generation. Tokenization in sports, although a relatively nascent concept, is strongly poised for expansion and innovation in the coming years.

10.1. The Vision: More Power to Fans

Tokenization has the inherent potential to place fans, not just at the periphery of the sports ecosystem but at the center of it. So, a future where ardent followers could influence club policies, elect leadership, and major decisions is not far-fetched. Just as the trends of popular vote-based reality shows and direct-to-consumer content platforms became the new normal, a similar shift in the sports industry, enabled by token systems, can become the predominant paradigm.

Fans could assume the roles of shareholders, stakeholders, strategists, and patrons, giving "power to the people" a whole new meaning. Sports communities grow stronger with collaboration and shared values, and blockchain tokens promise a future where everyone's opinion indeed matters.

10.2. The Paradigm: Reinvented Revenue Streams

One of the direct benefits of stepping into a tokenized sports industry would be the possibility of exploring a myriad of potential new revenue streams. Traditionally, the revenue-making avenues were limited to ticket sales, merchandising, broadcast rights, and corporate sponsorships. However, token systems could open up novel possibilities, such as in-game assets, digital collectibles, player trading, and many more.

Imagine a world where loyal fans make a little profit because their most loved player scored, their favorite team won, or simply because they held team tokens for a certain period. Fractional ownership and decentralized finance models can bring this to reality, providing a sense of belonging to the fans and additional revenue to the teams or leagues.

Further, non-fungible tokens (NFTs), which validate digital asset uniqueness, are expected to skyrocket in popularity for myriad applications like ticket sales, autographed memorabilia, player performances, etc.

10.3. The Game-Play: Heightened Fan Experience

While a fan's passion cannot entirely be quantified, tokens offer a valuable way to capture the allegiance and dedication towards their teams. Using tokens, it's possible to measure fan engagement on a new scale altogether—merchandise purchases, in-stadium activities, social media participation, and more.

On top of it, fans can be rewarded for their undying support. Their tokens can be spent on exclusive benefits—priority access to matches, member-only forums, meeting their favorite players, and more. Picture a stadia where the most dedicated fans cheer their teams from the stands, not because they could afford expensive tickets, but because they earned it through their passion.

10.4. The Ambition: Predicted Future Developments

In the upcoming years, technology and regulation are expected to mature hand-in-hand to allow the safe and wide-scale adoption of tokenization. In the near future, with improved regulatory safeguards, digital currencies and tokens would be accepted globally for in-stadium transactions, merchandise purchases, and even player contracts.

On the technology side, faster blockchains with better stability and even more transparency will emerge, which could further cement the credibility of token systems. Blockchain oracles could interact real-time with the physical world, and smart contracts could then action the outcomes instantaneously—making in-play betting, second-by-second trading, dynamic pricing, and fraud detection possible on a never-seen-before scale.

The impending years will witness more mature applications of tokenization in sports. There will be constant refinement and improved reflexivity according to the fans' behavior, changing market dynamics, and evolving regulatory environments.

10.5. The Conclusion: A Race, Not a Destination

The future of sports tokenization is not a static goal but a continuous evolution. As each day, new user habits are discovered, fresh possibilities unravelled, and previously unnoticed issues are put under the spotlight. This constant discovery will drive innovation, pushing token systems to be faster, safer, more transparent, and more valuable to stakeholders.

Just as the emergence of the internet caused a paradigm shift in how sports content was consumed—enhancing not just the reach but also interactivity—tokenization and blockchain are ready to morph the sports landscape again. They promise to redefine not just the economic of sports but also the very fabric of engagement and loyalty.

While it is imperative to navigate through significant challenges like regulatory uncertainties, technological limitations, and adoption barriers, the potential benefits of tokenization in sports far outweigh these hurdles. This game-changing evolution signifies an unprecedented shift in the sports industry, etching a promising future where power, influence, and profits are decentralized to the true heroes of sports - the fans. Welcome to the future of sports—tokenized.

Chapter 11. The Playbook Reimagined: Balancing Tradition and Innovation in Tokenized Sports

Tokenization, a product of blockchain applications, is revolutionizing nearly every industry, involving assets as different as art, real estate, and recently, sports. While tradition and modernity often find themselves in conflict, in the case of sports and blockchain, the situation is vastly different. The sports industry seems to have welcomed blockchain and its byproduct—tokenization, effectively integrating them into its core without usurping the integral traditional aspects.

11.1. Seizing the Ball: Introduction to Tokenization in Sports

In essence, tokenization involves the vivid conversion of rights to an asset into a digital token on a blockchain. This technology provides an open ledger for transactions, enabling increased transparency, security, and efficiency. For the sports industry, such a capability holds promising potential, from athlete contract tokenization to decentralized betting, enhancing fan engagement and even opening up new ways of funding.

The rise of fungible tokens (like cryptocurrencies) and non-fungible tokens (NFTs) portray a digital renaissance within the sports sphere. NFTs, unique digital assets, are particularly getting the highlight due to their potential to create unique, unduplicable tokens—that can represent fan merchandise or digital collectibles. This presents a remarkable opportunity to composite physical sports with digital value, providing a platform for a more interactive and immersive fan experience.

11.2. The Traditional Playbook: Conventional Forms of Sports Financing

Historically, methods of financing sports teams and leagues span a spectrum that includes private investments, bank loans, and IPOs. Despite their efficiency, these traditional forms attract several limitations such as high costs, paperwork, low liquidity, among others. Thus, teams often find themselves tangled in regressive debts and unfruitful financial structures.

As per the traditional playbook, fans interact mainly through merchandise sales, ticket purchases, and viewership, with no direct claim to assets. This limited interaction often dilutes fan enthusiasm, reducing their participation in the sport's financial cycle. Essentially, spectators have had to remain just that - spectators.

11.3. Breaking the Mold: The Introduction of Tokenization

The advent of blockchain in sports offers a divergent path from traditional financing methods. This new avenue promises significant advantages, including high speed, increased transparency, reduced costs, and, notably, the opportunity for fans to participate directly in the sports economy through ownership of tokens.

An example of this vision in action is how some football clubs have started issuing tokens. These tokens give holders voting rights on club decisions, similar to shareholders in a company. They also enable fans to participate in meet-and-greets, access VIP experiences, and acquire exclusive content. These features, in-turn, introduce unconventional revenue streams for sports clubs and increase fan engagement and loyalty.

11.4. A New Game Plan: Practical Applications of Tokenization in Sports

Tokenization has found multiple applications in the sports world. Paris Saint-Germain (PSG), Juventus and other top global football clubs have adopted tokenization to enhance fan engagement. Notably, these fan tokens enable holders to have a say in certain club decisions - including uniform designs, team anthem, friendly match locations, even selecting players for charity games.

Tokens have also found their way into sports merchandise, where they are backed by real-world assets like signed jerseys, footwear, and equipment. These tokens can be traded on platforms, enhancing their value to fans and creating a new revenue stream for teams and athletes. Manchester city, a pioneer in this area, has issued a series of digital collectibles and limited edition artwork as NFTs.

The implementation of tokenization extends to sports betting as well. Blockchain-based betting platforms offer fans a chance to bet on game outcomes using cryptocurrencies, offering secure and quick transactions, thus adding another fascinating aspect to the sports experience.

11.5. The Offside Rule: Challenges in Sports Tokenization

Despite the inspiring progress, it's important to acknowledge that tokenization in sports does not entirely sideline traditional methods.

Legal, regulatory, and technical challenges have to be considered. Regulations around blockchain and cryptocurrencies remain ambiguous in many jurisdictions. Alongside, questions surrounding the protection of token-holder rights are still unanswered. Plus, the technical intricacies of blockchain technology may seem daunting to non-tech savvy fans.

Moreover, the volatility associated with cryptocurrencies might pose drastic financial risks to both fans and clubs. As such, these challenges call for legal and regulatory bodies to adapt swiftly and constructively, developing blockchain-friendly frameworks.

11.6. Wrapping Up the Game: The Future of Tokenized Sports

Looking ahead, the confluence of tokenization and sports holds the potential to write a new playbook. This can bring about a profound impact, strengthening the relationship between teams and fans, giving birth to unexplored financial opportunities, and revolutionizing sports engagement. The road ahead demands amendments to existing legal frameworks and public understanding of blockchain technology. Yet, with steady advancements and the global technological zeal, the implementation of tokenization in sports seems not just viable, but inevitable. The idea makes clear that the beauty of sports is not in stagnation, but evolution. The metamorphosis may not be swift, but the result—a more inclusive, profitable, and engaging sports ecosystem—will be worth the wait.

In the end, the wholesome integration of tokenization in sports isn't about replacing the traditional playbook—it's about adding innovative chapters to it, pushing boundaries to reimagine it. The game is indeed on for tokenized sports with a potent promise to remake the sports arena in ways we've never seen before. Certainly, the tokenization wave is here to stay, not merely as a novel interlude but as an integral component of a grander digital era in sports.